Rural Places

Katie Peters

GRL Consultants,
Diane Craig and Monica Marx,
Certified Literacy Specialists

Lerner Publications ◆ Minneapolis

Note from a GRL Consultant
This Pull Ahead leveled book has been carefully designed for beginning readers. A team of guided reading literacy experts has reviewed and leveled the book to ensure readers pull ahead and experience success.

Lerner Publications Company
An imprint of Lerner Publishing Group, Inc.
241 First Avenue North
Minneapolis, MN 55401 USA

For reading levels and more information, look up this title at www.lernerbooks.com.

Main body text set in Memphis Pro 24/39
Typeface provided by Linotype.

Photo Acknowledgments
The images in this book are used with the permission of: © esvetleishaya/iStockphoto, p. 3; © fatihhoca/iStockphoto, pp. 14, 15; © Helga Madajova/Shutterstock Images, pp. 10, 11, 16 (horse); © McIninch/iStockphoto, pp. 6, 7, 16 (barn); © naramit/Shutterstock Images, pp. 4, 5; © SimplyCreativePhotography/iStockphoto, pp. 12, 13, 16 (tractor); © smereka/Shutterstock Images, pp. 8, 9, 16 (cow).

Front cover: © Ron and Patty Thomas/iStockphoto

Library of Congress Cataloging-in-Publication Data

Names: Peters, Katie, author.
Title: Rural places / Katie Peters.
Description: Minneapolis : Lerner Publications, 2020. | Series: My community | Includes index. | Audience: Ages 4–7 | Audience: Grades K–1 | Summary: "Engage and delight emergent readers with the sights of the farm. This title features carefully leveled nonfiction text and full-color photographs. Pairs with the fiction title I Look Up"— Provided by publisher.
Identifiers: LCCN 2019045799 (print) | LCCN 2019045800 (ebook) | ISBN 9781541590137 (library binding) | ISBN 9781728403021 (paperback) | ISBN 9781728400587 (ebook)
Subjects: LCSH: Rural development—Juvenile literature. | Land use, Rural—Juvenile literature.
Classification: LCC HN49.C6 P438 2020 (print) | LCC HN49.C6 (ebook) | DDC 307.1/412—dc23

LC record available at https://lccn.loc.gov/2019045799
LC ebook record available at https://lccn.loc.gov/2019045800

Manufactured in the United States of America
1 – CG – 7/15/20

Contents

Rural Places

Here is a field.

Here is a barn.

Here is a cow.

Here is a horse.

Here is a tractor.

Here is a farmer.

Did You See It?

barn

cow

horse

tractor

Index